Leadership to the Max 🐾

GENE HOWELL

Leadership To The Max

Published in 2017
by Gene Howell

Book cover design and layout
by Publicious Pty Ltd
www.publicious.com.au

Catalogue-in-Publication details available
from the National Library of Australia

ISBN: 978-0-646-96610-6

Table of Contents

Foreword...

One of our maxims at Leadership Western Australia is that we all have the capacity and promise to be great leaders, even though we might not carry the title of CEO or Managing Director. Whether in the family, classroom, community organisation, or workplace, each of us can take on the challenge of modelling courageous leadership and making our world a better place.

And yet, sometimes the whole concept of "leadership" can seem daunting and intimidating. We all at times suffer imposter syndrome, in which we question ourselves as to whether we are really qualified to be in the positions we are in. We all sometimes feel like we just don't know where to start, even when we are clearly in situations that we know require us to step up and lead.

My own thoughts about leadership are grounded in the concepts that great leaders "Just say Yes," and take on challenges, even when they sometimes feel out of their depth.   They are confident – not to the point of arrogance, but they have a deep belief that their good intentions, energy, and intelligence can create successful outcomes. Talented leaders show empathy, both for the people they work with and serve, and for themselves. And, to be a leader is, by definition, to be resilient. Not everything will work the first time. Our plans often get derailed.   A leader picks herself up, dusts herself off, and starts all over again.

With those thoughts in mind, I am honoured to be able to introduce you to Gene Howell and his dog, Max, who provide us with a down-to-earth approach to thinking about leadership. As Gene takes us on a tour of the garden with Max, or encourages us to lean down and tickle his pet's tummy, we move closer to incorporating some of the lessons from great leaders, including a great leader who was only about a foot tall and whose bark was definitely worse than his bite.

Robin McClellan
CEO
Leadership Western Australia

From the author

I have been learning about and talking in the leadership space for a long time, like over 40 years or so. Some 14 years ago we bought a dog, although my wife insists he's only 12 – he's been 12 for the past few years now, and the other day when someone asked how old he was she told them 11.

Over time – some 14, 12, or 11 years – I came to the realisation that our dog displays the characteristics that leaders need to display, he just does it much better.

His name is Max, hence the title.
Gene Howell

The characteristics of a leader 🐾

There are many books about leadership and they all express different things about what a leader should look like, how they should act, and how they should lead people. Most of these books are great but they lack one thing – they lay down the principles or ideals and tell you that if you follow those principles or ideals, you will be a good and successful leader.

The problem with this approach is that there is a difference between what makes a good leader and what is displayed in leadership generally. Often the books tell you the ideal, and that's the problem – we don't live in an ideal world and most of the people a leader has to lead are real, rather than ideal, including the leader!

The 29th President of the USA, Warren Harding, is a good example of this. Harding was persuaded to run for Presidency by his friend and political insider Harry Daugherty. The reason Daugherty wanted him to run? Because he 'looked Presidential'. That was it. He looked Presidential. Not because of policies, or great speeches, but because he looked Presidential. And because he looked Presidential, he was elected.

Harding has been recognised as one of the worst Presidents to ever hold office, and his administration as one of the top three most corrupt administrations ever in the US. In fact, it would seem that even his wife didn't like him because he was having so many affairs! He died suddenly whilst still in office – people have always suspected that his wife poisoned him, she ensured that when he died his body was cremated immediately before an autopsy could be done.

So Harding looked the part, acted the part, but was a terrible leader. Looks aren't everything after all.

The other problem of course is that a leader is also human. This means that we have to take into account that different people will react differently in different situations and there is no one solution that fits all situations. In one situation, you might apply a suggested solution and the people around you react the way you think they should; in the same situation with a different group of people around you, you might apply the same suggested solution that you tried before and discover that you have offended people, or that they resent you, or they don't want to do what you suggest.

Barry Posner and James Kouzes are two American Professors who have written a terrific book called "The Leadership Challenge". They identify what they call the Five Practices – note that, practices rather than principles – their comment being that these are things to *live* rather than things to *know*.

You see, we can know a lot about leadership. We can study the theory of leadership and we can create great principles of what great leaders do. But unless we actually live what we believe, it will achieve nothing.

Leadership is more about *being* than it is about *knowing*….

So I do agree with all the different writers out there that a good leader needs to hold close to the heart such things as integrity, honesty, the ability to inspire people, the ability to get people on board through relationships rather than telling them what to do, and so on. However, a great leader needs more than that.

And some leaders are the most unlikely people you would have ever thought would be a leader.

And that's what this book is about.

This book will not tell you how to be a great leader. It won't give a 1, 2, 3... of what to do. Why? Because I don't think that there actually is a 1, 2, 3 for leadership. We're all too different, so in this case, one size does not fit all. There really is no such thing (in spite of what people might say) as a 'profile' for the great leader; there are characteristics, there are possibilities, there are attitudes, and so on – but no 1, 2, 3 and now you're a leader.

The other thing we need to realise is that leadership may be for a long time, it might be for a lifetime, but for many of us it might only be for a season – a one-off event for which we take (or are given) responsibility.

Let's go on a leadership journey....

Leaders listen to the inner voice.

Sometimes we will be sitting in the lounge room, Max is in his basket, then suddenly his ears prick up and he starts barking and rushes to the front door or back door. We might get up and see what has made him react, but often there seems to be nothing there. "Stop your barking!" we say sternly, and he always has to have the last bark. What has happened?

He has listened to his inner voice.

Something inside him has heard a noise or sound, or some inner instinct kicks in and off he goes, the knight in armour responding to the challenge of a possible dragon.

Leaders need to hear and respond to the inner voice even when no-one else hears it.

I was listening to the radio the other day and heard this story. On August 13, 1955, Peter Hillary, Sir Edmond Hillary's son, was climbing in a group of eight on what is called the K2 mountain (between China and Pakistan). This mountain is more dangerous than Everest, and 'kills' one in four climbers who reach the summit (or at least that's what it says on Google). They had climbed to within a few hundred metres from the top and had paused before heading on to the finish. But Peter had a bad feeling about the weather. A little voice said to him "Go down, go down" and his father's voice came to him as well, telling him in his head to trust his intuition or gut feeling.

He told the others he was going back down. The others decided to continue their climb.

A huge storm hit as Peter was descending, and he barely made it back to camp. The next day was full of blue skies and clear weather as they waited to hear from the rest of the group. They never did. The other seven members of his group died in the storm.

What if?

What if he hadn't listened to the inner voice, that gut feeling?

Good leaders listen to their inner voice. They don't allow peer pressure to destroy or negate that little whisper or that nagging feeling.

Peter had more than enough training and his father had brought him up to listen to those moments and heed them. All of the group were experienced climbers, yet only one listened to the inner voice.

Sometimes when you are with others, it's easier to go along with the group, the general 'feeling' at the time. That's peer pressure. In larger groups, it becomes mass hysteria.

Peter Hillary had developed his skills and knowledge. He trained for it. He lived for adventure. He looked at pictures of the mountain, the paths, watched film of others climbing the mountain, listened to what they said. More importantly, he lived in an atmosphere of learning from his father.

Leaders don't rush into situations that could turn out

to be dangerous because they didn't plan, didn't have the skills, or didn't have access to the knowledge.

Learn from this. Plan, plan, plan. Listen to those who have been there before. Swallow the pride and listen and learn. Talk to people who have gone this way before.

Develop the ability to listen to your inner voice. More times than often, it's right.

Leaders are open to their followers — they don't hide who they are 🐾

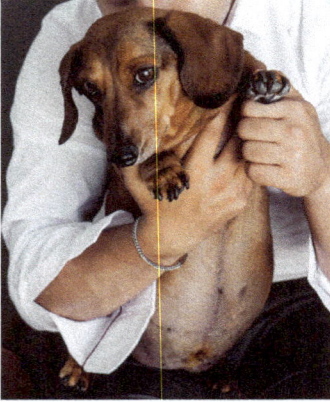

If Max were a human, he'd be embarrassed by this picture. He has no pants on and all is revealed. It's not a pretty sight.

Does he look worried? Embarrassed? Upset? Nope, because he's not. When he wants a tummy tickle, he rolls over onto his back, legs into the air, and who cares (from his point of view) if you see more than you wanted to?

Max's attitude is: take me as I am.

Leaders need to have the same attitude. "Here I am, this is me, take me as I am". That means the good as well as the bad. It's not about making excuses so you don't have to change; it's about recognising that none of us are perfect, but that that doesn't stop us from being a leader.

Some leaders try to pretend they are perfect. Some leaders are one thing when they are in front of the crowd, and another when you are one-on-one with them or when they are with a different crowd. Of course, the problem is what happens when all these different people are in the same place at the same time with that leader.

It's about integrity.

We've all heard of Donald Trump. The star of "The Apprentice" became famous for the words that everyone was waiting for at the end of each episode when he looked at one person and said: "You're fired!". In 2016 he was romping through America as the Republican favourite for President of the USA.

"The Apprentice" lasted 14 seasons. You tend to see Trump usually about twice during an episode, three times at the most. At the beginning of the episode he sets a challenge and either rings the contestants or connects via video conferencing or Skype. You may hear or see him again connect with either the contestants or the people for whom they are doing some work. You then see him again in the infamous board room where he will fire someone.

The problem with Trump is that he says things with so much conviction and confidence that people believe him. I am not sure whether he says what he really thinks or says what he thinks people want to hear. He somehow seems to have the ability to make claims, make promises, make accusations that are larger-than-life and often seem to go unfulfilled. Things like *"Let's build a wall between America and Mexico. That'll solve our unwanted illegal immigrant problem and we'll give Mexico the bill".*

On the other hand, Sir Richard Branson is a good example of a leader with integrity. I know that some people love him, some people hate him, but he is a *great* leader, not just a good one.

He also had a television show called "The Rebel Billionaire" which saw people working in groups, similar to Trump's set up. Here is the difference – Branson was with the group all the time. When they went somewhere around the world (using Virgin Airlines of course) he rode with them in the plane and he was with them when they attempted the various challenges he had set up.

Instead of the groups working in isolation (as was the case with Trump's groups), the groups would be together seeing how each other went. They would even have dinner together at the end of the session and talk about the day and their experiences - and Branson was with them. At times, he would even do some of the challenges or part thereof telling the group that he wouldn't have asked them to do something he was not willing to do himself.

His show only lasted one season of 12 episodes.

I think the reason for this was that he was too nice. He showed an integrity and genuineness, and that came through in all the episodes. Trumpet had no need to show these characteristics, as you only saw him for a very short time in each episode, and really, the teams do not work from a base of integrity or genuineness.

So here's the difference that you would see in the groups.

With Trump's groups, you see infighting, backstabbing, people disassociating themselves from the very person leading the group, and doing everything they can to undermine the other group, all in an attempt to prove they are the better person who should work for Trump (that being the end prize). Even the leader of each group is aware that the others in his or her group are hoping that they will fail so that they can take over and prove that they are better.

In Branson's groups, you see the opposite. People laugh together, they choose their own leaders and sometimes choose a leader from the opposite group. Each group watches the other group perform the challenge and actually supports them and encourages them as they go about the assigned tasks.

If a leader acts (for example) with true integrity, you will soon see the team begin to reflect the same characteristics. The reverse is also true.

Part of this integrity is a case of "what you see is what you get". Really great leaders are aware of their flaws and they don't necessarily hide them. They don't flaunt them, but they recognise their own weaknesses. This is not a case of displaying their dirty washing and being proud of it, but rather a case of being honest and admitting that I actually do have dirty washing.

Don't go overboard on this. This doesn't mean that everything has to be revealed. It's only in the past few years, for example, that Branson has introduced his son Sam. His family have tended to be kept out of the public eye not because Branson has anything to hide but because great leaders don't have to flaunt their private life in front of everyone. Branson is the first one to admit that he is not perfect; he is quite open about the fact that he doesn't have some of the skills required to run some of the companies associated with his name. He simply hires the people who do have the skills and knowledge required.

Trump comes across as arrogant and a know-it-all. He is loud, outspoken, and often brash. Branson comes across as quiet, sometimes outspoken, often makes big claims, but never comes across as arrogant or rude. Big difference.

"I made a mistake" is one admission a great leader needs to be able to make. It is what comes next that is important, and that is "so let's move on".

Made a mistake. I apologise. This is me. What can we learn. Now let's move on.

Integrity. Some have it, some don't. Great leaders do.

Great leaders
check out their
surroundings 🐾

I enjoy watching Max when he goes outside. He has a routine he pretty well follows every time. He climbs out the door and then stops for a few moments and sniffs the air. He's checking out what or who is around. Then he walks on to the brick paving just near our kitchen. He heads towards the plants in four large pots and walks behind them alongside the fence. He then walks onto the limestone paving and sticks his nose against a small hole that has been drilled in the fence. That hole opens into our neighbour's backyard and even though it is quite small, I guess he is checking for any unusual smells and making sure nothing has changed since last time. He then walks down alongside the fence and comes around our outdoor table and chairs. He then has two choices, either to walk towards the decking or head back to the door which he had exited a short time before.

Along the way, he may well have chosen a spot where he does his 'business'.

The only time he changes the routine is if he is in a real hurry to get outside and go to the toilet. However, once he has done that he goes back into his routine.

How many people do you know who simply rush in and do what they have to do without checking what's going on around them? Sometimes it's because their surroundings have become so familiar that they no longer see them. That means if something has slightly changed they just don't see it. That can be the pathway to failure.

Have you ever left work to go home and when you get there you actually can't remember whether some of the traffic lights you went through were actually green? You just can't remember going through that traffic light. You know it is there because you travel that route every day, but because it has become common to you and part of your environment, it doesn't grab your attention and you are on automatic pilot.

A good leader leads their people in the right direction and they don't go onto automatic pilot. If they are going somewhere they have never gone before, they check it out. They make sure that the team is going to be safe. But that's not a great leader. A great leader checks out where the team is going and where they are leading the team every time, even when they have been there before.

Now that may sound a waste of time. Why check out where you have been before when you already know what is there? Why? Because things may have changed.

I was once in a car rally as the driver. I had a group of younger guys in the car with me. As we headed down one particular road, one of the guys reading the directions said to me *"You better slow down as I'm not sure where this goes"* to which I replied *"It's OK, I've been here before".* And it was true, I had been here before.

But not that recently.

Since I had been there, they had changed the layout of the road, which I didn't realise until I turned the corner just before the end of the road. What had once been a one-way road had now become a two-way road and to my horror I was driving straight towards another car coming at me from the opposite direction.

I was lucky. I was able to move out of the way of the other car. But you get the point. I had been there before, I was going there again. I assumed nothing had changed.

I almost caused an accident, and someone could easily have been seriously hurt.

A lot of athletes have certain traditions they do before they go into the game. Sometimes it's a particular pair of socks that they wear; sometimes it's the lucky charm they have around their neck; sometimes it's picking up a bit of the dirt and grass and throwing it into the ear before they kick the ball.

This is not what I am suggesting. This is not about a lucky charm, or a tradition. This is not about going around and rechecking the doors and windows to make sure I locked them before I leave the house even though I have already checked them.

This is about caring enough to make sure your team is safe.

You are the leader, you are responsible. It's no good saying "Well, that wasn't there before!" as you watch a team member flounder or suffer failure. You should have checked it out to ensure that nothing has changed since the last time you were there.

So set yourself a routine. Follow Max's example. No matter how many times you have been there before you have a responsibility not only to yourself but also to the people who follow you.

Yes, it takes time to check out the surroundings. Yes, it can seem an awful waste of time seeing you 'know' because you've been there before. But you only need one significant change in the surroundings when you're leading your team that could cause disaster, simply because you didn't check it out.

We look out the window and see Max going through his routine and we laugh.

Who cares if someone laughs at your routine, at your checking the 'surroundings'? If this helps create great leadership and a highly successful team that achieves above and beyond what the average team achieves, you will soon have people knocking on your door to find out the secret of your success.

Ignore the laughter. Create the routine. And win.

Great leaders have special people they turn to for support

When I was writing the last chapter, something happened. Max was outside and chewing a chicken wing when a piece broke off and lodged in the upper roof of his mouth. He was coughing and spluttering, and beginning to froth as his body fought to get it out. I raced out and tried to help, but he wouldn't open his mouth properly for me to get it, and at the moments when he did, the piece of bone was too wet with his saliva to grip and pull out. We had an unexpected trip to the vet, my son driving the car and Max on my lap, trembling as I held him tight to calm him down.

Now and again he would look at me with his really sad eyes, wanting me to do something about it, even though I couldn't. That made me realise that there are times when he is not well, or he has an ear infection, or whatever – at these times, he will come and hang around me and just look at me as if I should be able to magically know what the problem is. I think he knows that when he is well, my wife gives him the attention, but when he is not well, I'm the one who will fix it or find out what it is and then fix it or organise someone to fix it.

I am the special person he turns to when he needs that particular support, when things go wrong.

Good leaders have people they depend on, like-minded people who can help them through the hard times. On the other hand, great leaders have special people they turn to – maybe just the one or two – who they turn to not just because they are like-minded, but because they can support them when they need it.

These people are usually straight forward and honest with you, they say things as they are rather than telling you what you want to hear.

Leaders need such people around them. They may not be there all the time, but in times of trouble or upheaval, they are there, and the great leader knows that.

Sometimes this support person will come to you because they see you going somewhere you shouldn't be going, and they step into your life before you can truly mess it up. They will do this because they care about you – after all, it's no skin of their nose if you mess up, so listen when they come to you, because those moments are rare and beautiful moments of growth.

My suggestion here? Have more than one person to support you, because often people perform different roles in your life. There may be the person you can cry with when you are hurting, the person you can laugh with when things are going great, the person you can share intimate stuff with and they won't turn on you. Then there's the person you can share wild ideas with, the dreams and fantasies, and they don't look at you as if you have totally lost it….

These could all be different people, or they could be one person or two people who combine some of the above. Great if you find the one, but also great if you find the many.

Who is the special person or people in your life who are your support persons? If you don't have any, find at least one and cultivate that relationship.

Personal note: *I once had a friend who whenever I wanted to find out what I should do, I would go and ask this person what they thought – and then I would go out and do the opposite of what they said and I knew I would be doing the right thing! Everyone has their place and role to play....*

Leaders embrace diversity 🐾

Now this is an interesting one, and one you will find hard to believe. In fact, I can hear you saying as you read this "He's a story teller, he's making this up" but I am not.

Max embraces diversity.

We've always made Max a part of the family. I think that nowadays he thinks he is human. He likes to be around people. He loves opening presents. He loves food he shouldn't – like avocado, and tomatoes, and grapes and watermelon, and peach, and yoghurt and cherries and sardines and toast...the list goes on.

And he has a friend.

This friend visits most days, they don't get really together, but they hear each other. Here's the catch.

His friend is a magpie.

I kid you not. There is one magpie that comes and talks to Max all the time, usually in the morning. The magpie doesn't know the difference or that Max is a dog because there is a one-way security door between them. Max can see out but the magpie can't see in.

Well, this magpie warbles away to Max quietly, Max chuffs back now and again, and they carry on this conversation. The magpie comes right up to the front door. I don't know what they talk about, I'm just pretty amazed about this unique and strange friendship that is carried on, the two of them oblivious to the fact that they are different species.

That's a pretty good leadership trait. In this day and age, diversity is becoming more and more necessary as different cultures become a part of the Australian ethos, and good leaders adjust to that and embrace diversity. Great leaders, by the way, don't wait for it to happen, they welcome diversity.

So why should we embrace diversity? Because it gives us a richness that we would never otherwise have.

People from different cultures do think differently. Things that are important to us are not necessarily important to them. If we aim to own a home because we have bought into 'the great Australian dream' where everyone should own a home, we will think differently to the person who grew up in Brazil or Argentina, where you're never going to own a house – and when you get married there, you probably move in with your parents who just add a room onto the house, so you now live with three or four generations of family. That gives a different perspective.

Diversity changes our perspective. When I was in South Korea, for example, I wanted to go out and buy a few shirts because they were so cheap. I went to a famous department store (Lotte I think it was) and they had these great shirts for about AUS$7.00 each – wow, I thought, what a bargain! In Australia, the same shirt would have cost me AUS$35.00.

But the Korean group I was with were shocked, and they wouldn't let me buy them – to them, that was too expensive. They literally marched (or herded) me out of the store and took me to where they bought their shirts for about AUS$3.00 each! When I tried to explain that the $7.00 was really cheap they couldn't understand, it was beyond their comprehension. When we talked, I discovered that what I made per month, some of their peers took a year to earn the same amount. No wonder they were upset that I would squander so much money!

Diversity gives you a different perspective. Once you travel overseas, and as long as you don't just stick to your own group of fellow country travellers, you will have your eyes and heart and mind opened up to new ways of thinking and seeing.

Diversity also opens you up to new ideas, to looking at things differently. It helps create ways that maybe you couldn't see before.

When I was in England, I enjoyed going and looking at some of the really old churches that had existed almost from when time began (ok, bit of an exaggeration). One of these was York Minster, alongside York Cathedral. Now at the time I was there, churches back in Australia were working through the issues of seating, interior decorating, and other important issues like that.

The arguments were that you couldn't attract youth if the chairs were like hard benches in rows, or that the colour scheme was funeral-related, and so on. And the churches were very much into attracting youth at that time because they were losing numbers. Young people were drifting off in droves and the big questions was how we got them back.

So Churches set their seating up differently, brought in tables and set up clusters, removed old wooden pews (that was a relief anyway) and redecorated with curtains and flashing lights and sound systems.

Meanwhile York. The church there is listed as a National Heritage building – which means you cannot change one thing about it at all! Can't change the seating – and we sat in some old pews which were surrounded by a wooden wall and a little door that allowed access to the seating – that's how it was for the richer members who had their own 'reserved' section. These seats ran parallel to the central area where the pews faced forward.

Yet I have to admit, the service held that morning we were there was fantastic and meaningful, even though there were no tables and chairs in clusters, or funky curtains and so on. That's where I learned that the setting, whilst nice to have if you can, doesn't actually make so much of a huge difference.

It made me realise that diversity and culture really go hand in hand. Diversity is not just about looking different, it's also about thinking different, living different, acting different, being different. It's about the environment around us.

Over the past few years in Australia we have had an influx of different cultures coming into the country and thereby challenging and changing our values. What's important to one person may not be so to another. Let me give you an example.

I drive a car. Everyone in our family owns and drives

a car. Each of us has chosen which car we bought — mostly second hand cars, but we checked them out and bought what we liked and what looked good, quite frankly. And to start with, each weekend they got washed and polished and vacuumed. That does sort of die off after a while, but we still tend to give the occasional wash and wipe and cleanout.

I'm also conscious when I'm driving, making sure I don't hit the curb or side-swipe another car, and so on. Then I started to notice something — the number of people whose cars had dents in the back or in the side, or who had obviously driven too close to a fence or wall and you could see the long scrape on the side of the car — in fact I watched someone park in a shopping carpark the other day and literally embrace the car alongside it!

Why don't they take more care? I thought to myself. Who on earth taught them to drive? And then I realised something.

In the West, we see our car as a status symbol, something we are proud of, something we almost revere. If we do get a scrape or someone drives into us, we get it fixed as soon as possible, because we just can't drive around in a damaged car.

That's not how some groups of people see their car, however. A car to them is a means of transport, it is a means of getting from one place to another. You know, if you dent it, it wasn't planned but I'm not really going to worry too much about it, after all, it's just a thing, and people are more important than things.

That's a great value to have – not the denting one, but the realisation that a car is just a thing, and that people are more important.

Maybe we are making important the wrong things in our lives. Maybe diversity can change that.

Leaders learn from diversity. Great leaders embrace diversity and learn lessons from it. Leaders recognise that diversity is about differences. Great leaders recognise that differences are what make their team strong and vibrant – and successful.

Leaders need to be comfortable with who they are.

I was preparing for a School Seminar in the East and communicating with a friend who is organising this event. In the past we have used another book I have written called "The Game Plan" and I sent her a copy of what I was writing (this book) and asked if she would be happy using this instead as I thought it might generate more discussion. We have a humour that underlies pretty well every communication we conduct, and part of her reply was:

> "I liked your book 'Leadership to the Max' but feel it could have been improved if Max was a cat...oh well...Max can't help what he is...after all Leaders need to be comfortable with who they are..."

So I decided to add this in as a chapter of the book, because it is quite true! Leaders do need to be comfortable with who they are.

How do you become comfortable with who you are?

First you have to know who you are.

Marcus Buckingham is the author of several books, one called "Go Put Your Strengths to Work". There's a lot of clips of him speaking on YouTube. One of the comments behind this book is when he asks the question: why did your company hire you? Well, the fact is, your company hired you because of the strengths you displayed. When you were being interviewed, they didn't ask what your weaknesses were and say "Love this guy's weak areas, let's hire him" but they did look at your strengths and hired you because of what you could do.

Pretty well this is where Buckingham says we make a mistake – we get hired and as time goes on, we then start looking at our weak areas and attend training to try and fix these weak areas – and in the meantime our strong areas reduce. People start to say things like "He/she used to be good at...." so Buckingham is saying that yes, we can work on those areas that need improving, but don't ignore the very strengths that got you hired in the first place – in fact, look for ways to grow and increase those strong areas. Because that's what got you employed in the first place.

I think one of the worst things we do to ourselves in Western countries is that we compare ourselves to others around us. Not only by what they do, but also by how they look.

Why do we do this to ourselves?

In Spain, the old men sit around in the village square and drink coffee (or something stronger) and they are respected for their wisdom. Are they fit old men? No. Are they good looking old men? No. Are they rich old men? No. So why do people listen to them?

It's called experience of life, and the wisdom of the ages.

That's something we have lost here in Australia. We are so concerned about continuing the Peter Pan image (he never grew up) that we spend massive amounts of money to look good and feel good – and quite frankly, our suicide rate has never been higher.

We buy the latest gadgets, we drive the best car, we go into huge debt to own a house or apartment, we get the best clothes that make us look young....and miss the beauty of simply being.

I remember hearing a story of a young guy in an American High School in his senior year. It is apparently a true story; I have to trust the person who told me. This young guy was in love with one of the most popular and gorgeous looking girls, and he desperately wanted to go out with her, but so did every other red-blooded male in the School. Whenever he said "Hi" to her, she turned up her nose and ignored him, as she did to pretty well every other guy there. She didn't go out with any of them.

Then he heard a guest speaker at the School, this guy had a major disability, and he talked about having to accept his disability, knowing that it didn't make him lovely, it didn't make him popular, and in fact people got a bit embarrassed around him. One day, he realised how stupid he was, that beauty is only skin deep, but true beauty is what happens inside you. So he decided to stop worrying about how he looked, and trying to be cool, and just be himself.

So this Senior guy thought about it and realised how he had been sucked in by the values of his day, which he now realised were pretty worthless. And he decided to change.

The next day, he went to school dressed in these old jeans with holes in the knees and a grubby T-shirt (one of his favourites), and other students laughed and pointed him out. He didn't care.

So he's walking down the school corridor, and here come Miss Beautiful, the girl everyone wanted to know. She stopped and looked at him. Looked at his daggy clothes. She went up to him, put her hands on her hips, and said "What on earth do you think you look like?" to which he said "Who cares? I'm just being me". And from the moment, she became his girlfriend, and they later ended up getting married.

Why?

Because she knew that most of the guys wanted her for her beauty. She wanted to find someone real, and she found him in the most unlikely way.

He had become comfortable with who he really was, not trying to 'play the game' that others around him were playing.

Be comfortable with who you are. There's someone out there who wants you for who you are, not for who you are pretending to be. People are looking for someone to follow who is real – be that person.

Leaders need
to know when to
surrender🐾

Max is a dog and dogs are pack animals and hierarchical in pack structure. There is a top dog. The pack knows who the top dog is and he is the Alpha. They obey him.

So when Max came into the family, he worked out the hierarchy. I was the top dog for him because I trained him, I disciplined him, I told him off, I rewarded him, and so on. He learned to listen to the tone of my voice. My wife was next in line, he went to her for comfort and love, and he would protect her as well if the boys were messing around or teasing her – Max would spring to her defence. Our older son was then next.

Unfortunately, our younger son sort of missed out. Not that our younger son didn't love him or anything, just that that's how it went. Max saw himself as being next in line and then my younger son – so often he wouldn't obey him, he wouldn't go to him when he was called unless I said "Max! Go to Chase!" and then he would reluctantly and slowly go to him.

However, if we were messing around, Max would race to his basket and pull out one of his toys and race with it to Chase to play with. Chase was there for playing and that was sort of it.

At night time, Max might be lying on our bed and when I came to get him he would roll over with his paws in the air and look at me with a "Please leave me here" look.

When dogs lay on their back like that, it's a sign of surrender, an "I give up" sign, a recognition of a higher authority. All pack animals do it.

Leaders need to know when to surrender. We all have dreams, and things we want to achieve, and often we get to do them, but other times there are just barriers after barriers in the way, people digging their heels in, resisting the way we are leading, and you have to ask yourself: is this worth it? Am I going to achieve what I want to?

Sometimes you need to re-evaluate and make some decisions like:

- do I give up totally on this?
- do I put it on the back-burner for now?
- is doing this essential for me to do what I am called to do?
- what will be the impact on myself, others, the company, the rest of the group if I give up on this?
- should I give up on something that I really believe in, that I am really passionate about?

In another age someone wise said "Fight the wars you know you can win". In other words, he was saying that fighting a war you know you can't win is a worthless exercise, even if you think you are in the right.

Now I have mixed feelings about that saying. Although there is truth in it, we have to consider that we might want to fight for what we believe in, for what we know to be true.

Colonel Gaddafi had a strangle hold on Libya. He was a dictator. But there were people in Libya who fought a silent war against him. Many of them died in his torture chambers which were discovered after his death. But they fought for a truth – freedom.

That's a fight worth fighting for, even though it was a war they couldn't win. Some wars are worth fighting, and you have to decide which ones they are. But don't refuse the fight just because it's a hard one.

Max's final comment:
know when your
leadership is over 🐾

Well, this wasn't meant to be the last chapter, but it has become an add-on simply because of events.

Life happens.

As I was writing what I thought would be the last chapter (the one before this), we were hit with sadness – we came home and discovered that Max had simply laid down and died. When we left for work, he was his usual fun-loving self, and we left thinking nothing of it. No signs of illness, nothing. We did the usual things, and so did he.

But when my son came home, he found Max had died. He had obviously had a drink of water, and as he turned, his heart gave out. No pain, no lingering, just the final of all finalities.

One movie I love is "Mr Magorium's Wonder Emporium". It's a magical, fun-filled bizarre film on believing in yourself. Mr Magorium tells Mahoney he is leaving the store to her, and she asks where he is going. He tells her he is going to die. She is upset, but

Mr Magorium says to her:

"When King Lear dies in Act V, do you know what Shakespeare has written? He's written "He dies". That's all, nothing more. No fanfare, no metaphor, no brilliant final words. The culmination of the most influential work of dramatic literature is "He dies." It takes Shakespeare, a genius, to come up with "He dies." And yet every time I read those two words, I find myself overwhelmed with dysphoria. And I know it's only natural to be sad, but not because of the words "He dies." but because of the life we saw prior to the words. I've lived all five of my acts, Mahoney, and I am not asking you to be happy that I must go. I'm only asking that you turn the page, continue reading... and let the next story begin. And if anyone asks what became of me, you relate my life in all its wonder, and end it with a simple and modest "He died."

And that's what Max has done. The "He died" is simply the statement of his life well-lived, of a life that brought joy and fun and laughter and moments of anger and rebuke and playfulness and greetings at the door when we got home, and head on the knee wanting to be scratched and on and on. All of that happened before he died. The dying is simply the conclusion of a life well lived. That's evident in the fact that we do – and will continue to – miss him terribly.

There was no fanfare. No announcement. No sign at all that his time had come.

Leadership – great leadership – is about knowing when you have done all that needs to be done, and then stepping out of the scene, letting life go on, having achieved what you set out to achieve. Not (hopefully0 dying, but simply stepping back to let someone else 'take the reins'.

There is nothing worse than seeing someone stay in a position that is no longer relevant. No longer needed.

Or no longer wanted. Watching someone linger on when their use-by date has come and gone. It's about learning when to step gracefully out of the picture.

We will not always be needed, but will we know when the 'not-needed' time has come to stop leading and allow others to take their rightful place?

We should step back when:
- we have finished the task we set out to do
- we have taken what we were doing as far as we can
- we have raised up others to take our place and continue the journey
- our time is done
- the task is complete and need go no further

It's a wise person who knows when to step back or to step out of the picture.

In his book *"Next Generation Leader"* author Andy Stanley comments that he felt he had to do everything, he felt that was what was expected, and besides, he was following in the footsteps of his famous father and he had this image to live up to. Then he discovered something: you can't do it all. He discovered what for him was a great secret that released him from the pressure of being. He discovered that his role was to lead, but to also pass on the baton to others around him so that they could take up the challenge and continue what he had started. What surprised him was that when he stepped back, people came forward, they had been waiting for him to stop so that they could do some of the things he was actually struggling to do.

He was actually standing in the way of people who were waiting to become.

Sometimes, if we don't stop, if we don't step out of the picture (and this is not an excuse to drop the ball and blame others who don't pick it up and run with it), we could be blocking those who are ready and willing to pick up the ball and keep it rolling. It's about who would step forward and do what we can't, if only we allowed them the opportunity.

So here's the question: will you know when you have come to the end of your leadership? How will you know when it's time to hand over to someone else?

My suggestion? Work that out before you begin, then it won't be so much of a struggle when you get there. It won't be about someone trying to wrestle your hands off the wheel because your time has come and passed and you don't want to let go. Learn to create what I call 'bus stops' along the way – places where you can stop and see where you have come from, where you are, and where you are going.

Most of us struggle to give up our leadership role to someone else because we never planned to do so. That's a sign of bad leadership – actually, it's more a sign of potential dictatorship.

Plan. Then do.

Go gracefully into the night, knowing that you have left the way open for someone else to take on the task, to lead, to achieve, to become.

Best...way...forward...
ever.

Thank you, Max.

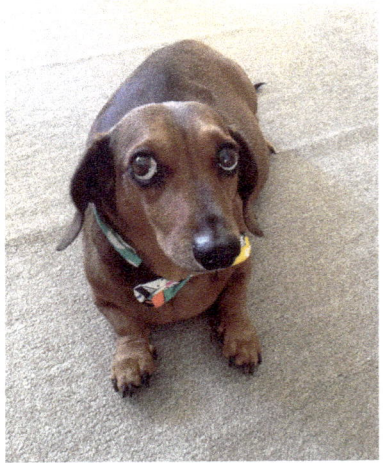